*a poem
for when
you need it
most*

*a poem
for when
you need it
most*

regan noelle smith

*Dedicated to Ricky and Rachelle—
for being there when I needed it most.*

Copyright © 2025 Regan Noelle Smith. All rights reserved.

This book or any portion thereof may not be reproduced or used in any manner whatsoever without the express written permission of the publisher except for the use of reprints in the context of reviews.

regannoellesmith.com

ISBN: 978-1-7376433-4-0

Cover design by Regan Noelle Smith
Edited by Katie Galloway

ATTN: SCHOOLS AND BUSINESSES
This book is available at quantity discounts with bulk purchase for educational, business, or sales promotional use. For information, please contact the author and team via regannoellesmith.com.

table of contents

A poem for when you…

…are hurting.   *pg 15*
May these poems help you know you're not alone.

…are grieving.   *pg 39*
May your grief be given a voice through these words; may they be a comfort and support.

…need a fresh perspective.   *pg 59*
Hope is here and the best is yet to come.

…are feeling joy.   *pg 89*
These words will celebrate with you.

…need to grow.   *pg 99*
A warm invitation, these poems will encourage and stretch you.

…need rest.   *pg 125*
May these poems prompt you to pause.

…crave awe.   *pg 137*
Because life is a great gift.

…are feeling (or seeking) gratitude.   *pg 161*
We'll share in this, together.

a letter to you, reader

Reader, this for you.

Whether I know your name or this is our first encounter—I want you to know I see you. I'm so grateful you're here. Not just reading this book, but here, in this moment, on this earth.

I know there are late nights when your body is exhausted but your mind won't rest. I see the awakening in your eyes when inspiration strikes. You've felt disappointment erode your spirit, and you've known hurt that crushed your hope—maybe more than once. Maybe it feels beyond repair. And still, you've endured. You've overcome immense pain. Though your heart may be bruised, blooms still grow from your fingertips.

This is where my affection for you begins—in the simple truth that your mind and mine are alike, even in all the ways they diverge.

Let me let you in on a small fragment of thought, but one that is an essential piece of the ever-expanding universe: you are deeply loved and have great purpose. Maybe this thought has been turned over in your mind, dissolving like a lozenge as you think through what this ambition entails. Or maybe you're waiting for it—your purpose—to unfold with patience as the future transpires. Maybe the word "purpose" tastes bitter on your tongue because this steeping thought is too overwhelming or grandiose.

Reader, even when we don't see eye to eye, I believe you are deeply worthy. Your life experience, perception, and perspective are uniquely yours, yet we're connected. You've never given up—you awoke from your slumber today, and all the previous days. Although you have been affected by hurt in the past and have experienced regret, you have conquered and continued.

I have a deep appreciation for the thoughts and emotions you carry—both the original and the tangled. Despite any distance in miles, background, or association, I am here as a witness. I offer my pen to write for you, this connection we share, and to invite conversation.

I spill ink onto this page to express my gratitude for you. Thank you for reading this letter. Thank you for showing up today, for others and for yourself.

As you sweep through the poems and notes within these pages, may they become your own. Our circumstances may not mirror one another's, but our emotions parallel. These words speak to what is sacred and shared between us. They will saturate deeper than the surface of your eyes; they will settle into your soul and put language to what feels impossible to express. You may just feel understood.

With boundless love,
Regan

A poem for when you are hurting.

May these poems help you know you're not alone.

a poem for when you are hurting

motion sick
—

Thoughts have been
rocking me back and forth;
a cyclone swirls in my stomach.
I'm a spinning top, trying to reorient,
correct, and balance, but my heart is
getting flung every which way;
I try to stand,
steady, still…
but am pulled into a tilt.
I tip and fall.

hollowness

My pain isn't any less
tolerable than yours.

The ache is immeasurable.

Each of our experiences are
unique to us, yet
we both have felt
our skin stretch and shred
as our hearts were ripped out
from between our ribs.

We both know the lonely echo
of other's words—
meant to bring comfort—
ringing out, instead,
with the sound

of our hollowness.

when you don't know why you're sad

—

These moments seem
to exist outside of time,
the sadness waiting to
be named by reason.

Yet this ache won't last forever,
so sit briefly with this cloud
of frustration, let it weigh heavy
in your lungs—allow your deep
sighs to bring you through as it
begins to pass.

The fog will lift in time.

vast
—

If you're sensing:
overwhelm,
a mind too rigid to wrap
around or embrace,
too claustrophobic to hold
space for, or if you feel capped
beyond your current capacity
to comprehend,

I invite you to take a walk with me.
Let's look at the sky together.

It may be:
overcast today, or
bright blue with billows,
an opaque black sheet, or
inky, but freckled with light.

Regardless of the weather or
time of day, notice how expansive it is—
how wide and deep.

Let's get lost in its vastness.
Take it in, and exhale your worries
here. There's space for it.

Let's linger.
Notice how the vastness
compares to the shrinking sense
of overwhelm.

Sometimes the weight of
reality feels heavy still.

a poem for when you are hurting

That's okay — some circumstances
bring loss and stir our grief.
You're not alone in this.

Move outside of the self and
see the magnitude, see everything
begin to align. Joy and grief,
neither exclusionary.

Watch worries dissolve when
they're brought to this eternal scale.

Soon the senses sync,
and this tangible display
prompts new perspective.

Soon the overwhelm
no longer seems too big to hold.

mental illness

All we ever do is fight,
you keep me up all night,
and I don't want to waste my time,
take your mind out of mine.

I wanna run away.

a poem for when you are hurting

numb
—

There are days
when all I want is to simply
slip away—escape what's
in front of me; whether it be
a memory
a dream
a heavy responsibility.

This is when I want to go numb.

When I want to numb,
my urge is to grab the bottle—
a motion my muscles still remember.
My urge is to revert back
to the days when I'd consume
and become consumed.

Going to bed drunk, and
waking hollow—ending up
with more burdens than I had before.

When I want to numb,
what my soul is really searching for
is surrender. To stop carrying
the backpack of rocks that's straining
my neck and leaving my body weak.

It's been years since I was a slave
to addiction, but I'm still having
conversations with my therapist
about slip-ups, urges, self-boundaries.

When I want to numb, I need to
drop the grocery bags of "shoulds"
that imprint red rings onto my wrists.

To accept kindness without suspicion.
There aren't attached strings meant to
tangle and trip.

I cover myself in prayer, accepting
His offer to carry the hardships
I don't have to call mine.

I'm a flawed human who will fail,
but am dedicated to full healing.

Even still,
my wholeness has never
been contingent on my effort,
but on my faith in who He is.

a poem for when you are hurting

decision-fatigue
—

My eyes feel as though
they are being pitted —
plucked from my ripe skin.

Questions blur before me
in a swirl so dizzying
I can't access
the clarity required
for an honest yes
or a sober no.

And though I've been
sleeping more than ever,
a tired grip pulls me deeper
than gravity could.

Decision-fatigue
is my self-diagnosis.

But realigning myself,
I make the only
essential choice:
to pause and recognize
that time will continue
past my personal eon.

All I must do is rest,
and let the urgency slip, too,
watching the sky slowly shift
from blue to a brief purple,
and settle into a deeper hue.

reminder
—

I hope you take the time,
to take care, too.

a poem for when you are hurting

permission to pause
—

Give yourself permission
to pause for a moment.
Close your eyes and breathe in
through your nose.

Breathe out; as you do,
relax your shoulders,
release your jaw,
let your lips slightly part.

Take in another inhale; let it
circulate within your consciousness
and clear out the day's distractions.

It may take a few breaths to
release your relentlessness.

Continue to ease into a pattern
of slow breathing.
With each inhale, expand
into a greater depth.
With each exhale, usher in
ease to the tension your body holds.

This might be the first time today
your mind hasn't been racing.
If it's hard for your mind to slow in
its pace; that's okay. Give yourself grace.

There's nowhere to be but here.

regan noelle smith

what i need to hear

I cannot tell you
I know exactly what
you're feeling, thinking,
or how you're hurting.
But I can tell you,
I'm here with no other
purpose, but to listen
and listen well.

*I promise not to think
of what to say next.*

a poem for when you are hurting

your past
—

My heart breaks
when you drop a word
within our conversation
that alludes to your past hurt;
while now, it's only a faint echo,
it still reminds us how the hurt
in your past was once
deafening.

regan noelle smith

a body, begging
—

Restlessness
fills my bones, my body
overheats from burnout.

Coffee is borrowed time, and
I'm severely in debt. The mirage
of productivity never served the
dead well, but it sure keeps me
distracted from sitting in silence.

Silence brings awareness, surfacing
pain I don't yet want to face.

Head tied tightly to my heart, my
temples beat with my pulse.
Heat sears overtop of my
eyes with each blink.

Even if I occupy my mind
with anything else, my body
still shows my past trauma;

hurt is:
held in my
furrowed brow,
in my clenched teeth,
in my tight shoulders,
upset stomach,
lack of appetite,
too much appetite,
sleeplessness,
oversleeping,

a poem for when you are hurting

and my body
begs me to mend.

inadvertently numb

I meant to quiet my heart,
not to make it stop beating.

a poem for when you are hurting

heartbreak
—

Loving a human
can shake the world to shambles.

Shards and slivers of glass
circulate, sparing no pain as my
heartbeat reverberates their shrapnel
throughout my entire body.

Heartbreak.

Though my vision is blurry
from somber sobs, I set my sights
on the divine act of Love that sent
seismic quakes through
the world,
the law,
death itself.

How wholly healing
Love is, He gathers
even the fragments—

Heartbroken,
He is near.

when you hold the hurt
too close

—

Undue responsibility
I confused for nobility
has caused calcium and limestone
to narrow my arteries.

Now,
I'm exhausted,
stressed, and out of breath
from holding
other's hurt too closely.

May this hard heart
soften through prayer
and surrender:
the myriad of responsibilities
that were never meant for me.

a poem for when you are hurting

healing is hard work
—

Healing is hard work,
and I realize I'm
regressing,
slowing to a standstill:

I've reached my
capacity of growth
and my former self
found the height of all
I'll ever achieve within
my healing journey.

The blessing is
none of that is true.

Every effort I make
to heal is progress,
and

the more time I
participate in self-reflection,
rather than pacify with distraction,
the more I find my blind spots.

Every time I practice
observing what's around me
instead of absorbing it,
I barter for more
mental clarity.

The more I listen,
the more I learn.

And,
the more I quiet myself—
finding stillness in my thoughts—
the more I truly hear.

Even in this quiet,
I feel a pull to be "productive,"
a push to produce and create
something I can be proud of.

But I am already
doing exactly that,
though it is not something
my hands can hold.

I'm allowing my mind
to be renewed,
to be made new.

I'm doing the hard
(and worthy) work
of healing.

a poem for when you are hurting

but he who heals
—

Some words said to me
(or that I've said to myself)
were baseless or distorted,
meant to tear me down to
protect a fragile ego.

These took form as:
a passing jab, a conscious
effort to thwart my potential,
a remark shared through the
lens of pain, since hurt people,
hurt people.

Some words stuck.
Their seeds of darkness
took root and grew.
And at times, I lashed out.
I replayed each encounter
until I was trapped in a shame cycle.
One can only withstand so much
self-hate before beginning to break.

I broke. And I broke open.

But in my most desperate moment
was when I was met with the most
                          patient love.

None of my hurt was erased, but I
no longer had to carry it alone.

Healing didn't start with a radical
mindset renewal. It started with

simple words of truth—a salve,
and genuine love—a balm.

The renewal of my mind was gradual;
the hatred I had for myself lifted
slowly. I was told I had worth, that
I was created on purpose, for a purpose,
for such a time as this—I was told I am
chosen, loved.

I received forgiveness.
And in that, freedom.

No, the hurt I went through was
not the purpose, but has been used
for good—allowing me to extend
empathy, understanding, hope.

My scars are evidence,
not that God hurts, but that He heals.

a poem for when you are hurting

A poem for when you are grieving.

May your grief be given a voice through these poems; may they be a comfort and support.

a poem for when you are grieving

many forms
—

You can be grieving—

the loss of a loved one,
a place, a past self,
life before trauma, or
the quiet fading of a friendship,
who someone once was,
who you once were,
unmet potential, and
dreams that never took shape...

Loss of any kind can stir something deep.
Let it be what it is—grief.

powerless
—

I close my eyes,
and black hole
after black hole,
I fall deeper;
and like a spaceman,
I have no control of the
elements around me—
I'm weightless,
yet simultaneously,
hauling a heavy shell,
floating with no gravity,
drifting further and further away
from all that I call home.

a poem for when you are grieving

mourning
—

The grief
that laid on my heart
was as sudden as the
shift from dusk to nightfall,
sand slipping quietly in
the hourglass,
now unmoving—

silence.

I wish we had more time.

regan noelle smith

i will see her, though
—

I keep thinking I'll see her—
sunbathing on the beach,
or lounging in a folding chair
beside the street market's boxes of
mangos, papayas, and bananas—
all matching her vibrancy.

I'll see her teaching students,
waving as they depart from the school yard,
their heads bobbing in unison,
their clothes, uniform. Maybe instead,
I'll see her driving their school bus home—
seems like a random job she'd enjoy,
for a time, bringing joy to little lives.

I keep thinking I'll see her—
but I know she's not here.
Not in Curaçao, Costa Rica, or Aruba.
Not in any classroom or yellow bus.

She's in a place I cannot yet reach.
My ache for her makes her manifest
like a dream in the scenes before me.

I keep thinking I'll see her—
and beyond this world, I will.
I wait, and one day, I'll join her
in the grand adventure of worlds unknown.

a poem for when you are grieving

grief
—

I find myself crying in
a workout class, then
fully happy, reading
memories written in old
journals, motivated to
express the grief and joy,
and in the next moment,
I'm lethargic and immobile.

Lines, corners, curves.
Laughter. Cries.

Shapeshifting —
to fit whatever shape
my grief takes today.

talk
—

Grieving is wanting to talk about it; grieving is not wanting to talk about it.

a poem for when you are grieving

a july 4, without fireworks
—

My shaky knees sit together,
with feet on the wall
propping me back into the posture-failing chair,
a few feet away from the hospital bed.

I peer out the blinds onto the small town,
saturated in the spill of afternoon sun;
my mind is a mixed-up ball of yarn,
a thread of thought that's been tumbled and knotted —
stature matching my stomach.

Low-quality recordings of familiar songs
meant to soften the rigidity of this foreign place
play, in the background, for her —
her airway, obstructed, offers the occasional gurgle,
and the throat humidifier moonlights
as a white noise machine.

My hummingbird heart hovers over confusion.
My half-open head fights with frustration.
I ache for her body — bones bringing tenderness
to the surface through pressure ulcers, skin now
thinner than the fabric of the hospital gown.

I twinge at every pinch and every needle,
though she isn't able to move a muscle.
I pray for her mind, fully functioning, yet
unable to form speech.

I breathe deep.

God's never left us,
and hasn't now.

He hasn't vanished for even a second
within this all-enduring wait; though we
wonder when this hour will be over.

He's in the humidified air,
bearing the cinderblock weight we all carry
and in the bright blue eyes of my mother-in-law.

He's there in our heavy hearts,
when the diagnosis offers months,
when doctors share the prognosis with
tears welling, when my soul feels shattered.

He's in the moments where her husband
feels peace—the kind that surpasses all
understanding. He's in the care the nurses
extend, in their patience and diligence.

He's holding us,
calming our minds,
holding our hearts,

even amidst the mess.

a poem for when you are grieving

grief again
—

Remembering only the good,
remembering only the bad.

regan noelle smith

unrefined words
—

How am I supposed to return to normal life? The grief is as fresh as the purple polish I swiped on my fingernails for my mother-in-law's funeral service.

I'm just a regular human who doesn't know what to do with grief: I say the wrong things with good intentions, I stuff and spill, misdirect my anger. I'm simply empty.

I work too late, distracting myself and avoiding writing at all costs. The outpour of helping hands and hearts offering to share in the heaviness is what's kept me from being crushed.

I'll never forget seeing our inverted reflections on the casket buckles in the cemetery. I guess it was a glimpse into what life would look like—a reality I recognize, but everything feels flipped upside down.

a poem for when you are grieving

feels like poison
—

Everything has fallen to pieces
and I'm trying to puzzle together
how this all came to pass.

To deconstruct grief is to
extract cream from coffee;
knowing what once was, but now
everything is muddled together and
my hands are helpless here.

i miss your morning greeting
—

Last night,
I had another dream of you.

You had blunt-cut bangs,
sharper than you'd like,
and the sight of you
made me cry.

You told me it wasn't you,
but I was sure of it—
matching mole near your cheek,
slightly beneath your nose.
I suppose my subconscious even
knows you're no longer here.

And I woke up, crying, begging
for you to be released from this hold—

to allow you to sit up,
sip some coffee,
and ask how I slept last night.

a poem for when you are grieving

breathe deeply again
—

I've been keeping my hands busy,
gripping the handle of rubber weights,
propagating plant cuttings and repotting,
lifting bites of this and that to my lips —
but not writing.

I've been remaining occupied:
diligently filing *diligent effort forms*,
reviewing code, ensuring process hygiene —
complaining and planning,
simultaneously over and under analyzing
my mental state; hesitant to allow my mind
breathing room or space.

But no amount of cramming my mind or
passing the time will soften this sorrow.

I need to give time and self-allowance
to heal, even though it hurts. To have heartbreak is
to have loved. To recognize the brevity
of our time here is an invitation to steward it well.

So I'll create and love and cry and let others in.
I'll forgive and hope and dream and while
the wind has been knocked out of my chest;
I won't expire from this breathlessness.
I'll write until I no longer have ink in my pen.

With one hand on my heart and the other
on my abdomen, I'll feel my rising chest
and breathe deeply again.

wasn't meant to be
—

Humans were never made to grieve. We weren't meant to taste death, to see a body without breath. We were meant to hold others close, to laugh until our stomachs ache while our cheeks turn rosy red. We were meant to grow gardens together, both fruit and memories. To run alongside the rushing river without worry of slipping in. We were meant to be continually filled with childlike wonder, plucking wildflower petals to throw as confetti, to share our most daring dreams, to be rooted in eternity.

Though her body no longer has breath, I'll hold onto the memories that made us both feel so alive.

a poem for when you are grieving

purple pansies
—

Outside,
across the incandescent sky,
the boreal chickadee bird dips and ascends,
a fluttering pattern with acute acceleration.

Inside,
a heartbroken husband,
speaks softly to his wife,
brushing a loose hair behind her ear,
gently kissing the top of her head,
as natural light shines and comforts,
warming her skin.

A mother who can see but not speak,
feel but not move—
but oh,
how her son sings for her,
strumming until blisters burst.

And her sister
places purple pansies in eyeshot,
plants a shepherd's hook outside her window,
hangs from it a glass cylinder
filled with seeds for the round-bellied robins,
the yellow-breasted chat,
and the cuckoo with its black bill.

And though her head lays heavy,
I hope her heart is heaping full—
for the beauty that unfolds
everywhere, even when the vessel feels broken.

grief is

Grief is standing in the rain to watch a bird
carry a branch along the sky,
asking to borrow a stranger's hotspot
to write a memorial poem
on your computer,
lying in bed until noon,
forgetting what day it is,
being void of emotion,
flipping through photo albums and
laughing with heartfelt joy,
using admin skills to plan a funeral,
arm wrestling to lighten the mood,
going on a walk to cry alone,
trying to be a professional while
fighting chronic cognitive fog,
sharing silent car rides,
remembering every detail,
being hyper-productive,
sobbing in your brother's arms,
accepting the generous gifts of
time, meals, floral arrangements,
disconnecting from nearly everything
because my heart can't handle anything else.

a poem for when you are grieving

you live in a place i can't visit
—

Sleeping yet
alive in eternity;
time is different in your realm.

And while I'll sob in the margins
of time, I have peace knowing
you're alive and well, though
no longer with us.

regan noelle smith

what lies beneath
—

Tides of time expose a blue
shoreline and rest uncovers
what has been lying beneath:
I miss my sisters.
I'd like more time with my mom.
I'm still learning to live
in the world with a loved one lost.

But I have the great luxury
and pleasure of existing
in this slice of space —
sitting with the waves,
no land in sight; a pelican
dips down into the water. I wonder:

How far from home does he fly?
How can I protect my boundaries?
How high are these waves?
How can I rest in what is, not
wallow in what I wish was?

Questions that stand
as monuments in my mind,
uncovering what lies beneath.

a poem for when you are grieving

the sun shines today also
—

Grief hangs,
but the days continue—
the linens need
to be folded,
the dog fed,
the dishes scrubbed.

I count each mundane movement
a small victory:
the sun shines on both
my grief and my needs.

A poem for when you need a fresh perspective.

*Hope is here and
the best is yet to come.*

a poem for when you need a fresh perspective

vibrant
—

My palms hold the
sunshine
of simple joys,
while grief hangs
heavy on my heart; gratitude
spills generously, as do
tears. Depression leaves
its mark while I savor the
goodness of God.

When things are quiet,
the otherwise hidden thoughts
and emotions emerge loudly.

As they surface,
I lean in with grace;
though they may contrast,
I don't allow them to compete.

Vibrant, messy, honest.
To have an amalgam of emotion

is to be human.

past & present pull
—

I've been feeling off balance lately,
pieces of my mind scattered across the long ago.

My summer skin is warmed by
the afternoon sun
beneath a butternut tree.

It's beautiful,
this patch of nature nestled
within the cityscape,
though I'm trying to recollect parts of my mind,
some subconsciously fastened to the past,
I'm trying to pull and pry them back
into the present's possession.

But I know I need to release my hold
and evolve into this new scene; I don't need
my whole life together
to have wholeness
here, where my story sounds
like a string of stuttered words.

I give compassion to others,
but find I rarely spare myself
breathing room or space
I crave control,
walk on through stress fractures,
placing too much weight on
myself and myself alone.
mixing today's fruit with yesterday's,
spoiling it all.

a poem for when you need a fresh perspective

Can I begin again?
Start a new season with
nothing owed to yesteryear?

*A prayer
beneath a butternut tree.*

molting
—

I'll move forward, no longer caught
in the grasp of my past self.

I'll endure the shocking shedding
of my

skin,
thoughts,
ideas,
memories.

this release, I trust, is a necessary step
in the quiet growth that calls.

a poem for when you need a fresh perspective

today

How precious is this
one life,
full of wonder,
possibility,
all hinging on
our very will.

While we may not have
yesterday
or tomorrow,
we do have today.

regan noelle smith

this sure sign
—

Art collaboration with Julia Signe during the ONE Artist Residency

I slow myself and settle.
My murky mind trudges through
the haze that's polluted my perspective.

But before me, a revelation ripens;
I begin to peel back the layers of intention—
the orange zest collects beneath
my fingernails as I dig deep,
dewy citrus drops burst like
fireworks in the golden sunlight.

I'm immersed in the rich color,
drawn in by the gentle
pulling apart of each piece,
joy illuminates—
and everything around me savors—

this sure sign.

a poem for when you need a fresh perspective

unceasing
—

My pothos grows new leaves;
they emerge from the vine, bound tightly
and unfold with a glossy green glint
that catches the sunlight.
Always in my line of sight, yet

I don't even notice.

May our prayers be the same—
growing so steady,
going unnoticed to ourselves, because
we're so close to it, because
we're living it; and while
it's quiet, and there's no great contrast,
it bears the evidence of

well-nurtured roots:
sustained and unceasing.

.

regan noelle smith

look at the birds
—

Black birds with tomahawks,
silvery blue feathers.

They call to us
to leave our worries,
a physical reminder that
we will be (already are)
taken care of.

a poem for when you need a fresh perspective

perennial joy
—

Thoughts flow through my mind,
fluttering like leaves within the autumn breeze.

My afternoon perch is lofty with fall's foliage,
cirrus clouds smeared against crisp blue canvas.

Beaming rays accentuate all—
regardless of whether I take shade within
the tree's outstretched arms.

I reside upon the park's grass—
this whimsical landscape,
living within the worthwhile.

But the sun's light could subdue blinding,
the breeze becomes bitter and the stones beneath
my crisscrossed legs turn sharp.

Temperament changing the temperature—
the bird's song becomes bickering,
the worthwhile, now wayward.

I wish to watch through the golden light,
how it filters through the hydrangeas,
peeking through the perennial ferns.

Monarch wings shimmy in the solar rays.
I'll be taken aback by this breathless beauty,
the cyclic serene standpoint.

For this composition will contain all elements,
foreground, middle and background—

but that which is distinct is the decision:
which point-of-view I choose.

a poem for when you need a fresh perspective

thought anchor
—

How can I feel euphoric,
and then crash in the next moment?
This rapid shift—cognitive contrast.

Whatever the circumstance,
I'm learning that to truly live means
accepting every moment,
each one equally part of my life:

Moments when my lungs fill
with saltwater air, my hand in my lover's.
Moments when it feels as if my soul
has left my body—yet aches within.

Though I rarely remember this
each day unfolds, each thought
carries the weight of a choice:
to observe or distract,
to hold on or let go,
to break down or build up,
or to shed an old skin
and welcome renewal.

Each passing thought,
a chance to choose.

regan noelle smith

it's never too late
—

Take a deep breath. You're okay.
The flood you feel now—along with
its ruin and damp disaster—will dry.

Keep working hard and finding rest.
Lay all your books open
in the sun. Read whatever words
you can make out and remember how time
has a way of shrinking the matter.

Will it still matter?
In two years, two months,
or even two weeks?

The weakness of the present is
its pitifully small perspective.
But its gift is placing you in position
to realign, shift, adjust.

Nothing is lost, not for long.
No ruin is unredeemable,
no experience wasted.
At any moment, breakthrough
is a breath away.

a poem for when you need a fresh perspective

living faith
—

Let me slow my script
as an intentional act of patience.
My mind reminds my body
even in my writing.

Living faith looks like
looking others in the eye,
creating space for conversation
even if only a few words are shared —
loving well and letting offenses fall.

To pause and give notice to
beauty often overlooked —
especially in humans — this
should be our heartbeat.

We have the ability to change our life,
the power to inspire change in another's.

What a shame it would be
if we moved through our days
without gratitude — without
recognizing every breath we take
is a gift, this expansion of our lungs
we should not take for granted,

for even in the bad,
there is still so much good.

columbus

Columbus met me
with full yellow blooms
and weepy grey skies.

She was once my patient mother,
when I had first arrived
and called her my home
six years ago.

She was gentle,
stroked my hair,
let me cry as I
healed from hurt,
and purely listened.

She watched me
get married,
taught me how
to steady my lifestyle,
and would sing me
lullabies in the thick
of the forest bed.

She let me leave,
sending me with
nothing but love.

During my absence,
I learned discipline —
firm teaching that
truth and love
should never be
untwined; rewarded

a poem for when you need a fresh perspective

with strength and
responsibility.

And now,
four years later,
I cross state lines,
landing back in
my mother's arms.

And while she's
thankful I'm coming
home, she knows
I'm not returning solely
as a daughter,
rather a mother myself.

I've fallen pregnant
with dreams and visions,
the beginning of a
lineage that will stretch
across the world;
and now I wait patiently
to give birth, saying
a prayer every morning,
preparing my mind
and my home.

And again, she's gentle,
as I ask how to nurse and
nurture these newborn
dreams which will
come to fruition,
and take full form.

seasons

Our lives are lived in seasons;
even the meadow across the lane
blossoms in its own time.

a poem for when you need a fresh perspective

garden of the gods
—

There was noise
around the size of my nose.
High school girls consumed
with the clatter.

I hid half my face
in every photo,
trying to adjust my attributes,
starving my body in efforts to
shrink my skin.

If only I would have had this view:
red rock skyscrapers that rise to the clouds,
tall grass swaying in the pockets of exposed earth.

The mountains don't modify themselves,
to suit the spectators.

My body was cosmically
created—a vessel for something
greater than this rock garden.

For my soul will last longer than stone.

regan noelle smith

but still beautiful
—

Life is messy,
but still beautiful.

Even when the mind is claustrophobic
from recurring responsibilities,
when the day demands productivity and
focus, while grief mounts and the
good feels frail —

it is still worth living.

You breathe purpose with each breath.
Between doing dishes and folding laundry,
fighting through brain fog and comparison —
you persevere.

And while you may not see the reason,
your resilience is penning a poem within
the ordinary hours.

Your presence is a refreshment to others —
a welcome reprieve from their day's challenges.

And in time, these days,
yours and theirs, will feel
brighter, your heart will feel lighter
and you'll get to sink your teeth into
the sugary-sweet apricot harvest
of the seeds you've sown
by *living*, as you are —
loved.

a poem for when you need a fresh perspective

regrets
—

Anything worthy of regret
has already been forgiven
and can be redeemed,
simply ask Him, and

allow yourself release.

hibiscus
—

I wonder if I retreat
inwardly too often—
as if there is a limit to self-reflection,
as if I'm a bud that blossoms
only to recoil again, trying to fold
my petals back into sepal leaves, hoping
to further grow before being on display.

But maybe that's the problem:
I'm the root, not the bloom—
my lifetime realization is not limited
to the floral incarnation.

I work underground, in unseen places.
Each lived-out piece of introspection
builds and may surface in bloom—
but I am not my flowers, nor my fruit.

My meditation and muse remain
the same: may I be a persistent
perennial—always rooted in You.

a poem for when you need a fresh perspective

gentle hope
—

I wake up again,
needing strength,
and You sit next to me,
offering it.

Hollow and grieving,
I receive the birds' songs
You bring to soothe me
as Your hand holds
mine tight.

When I feel cold and
withdrawn, You send the
sun to shine on my brow.

When there's too much noise,
You don't try to compete—
You offer a whisper of gentle hope.

anxiety
—

I take this feeling,
collecting it from my body,
mind, and spirit, and I press
it into a ball within my hands;
it's much heavier, denser,
but smaller than I had imagined.

And as I surrender it, the anxiety
separates from me—water from oil.

a poem for when you need a fresh perspective

it will

—

An ekphrastic poem in response to the painting Will It?, by Izaiah Miller

It will get better.
These sound waves
bounce off my skull,
never seeming to sink in,
no matter how many times
it's been said to me.

It will get better.
Will it?

I feel torn in so
many directions;
nothing feels safe,
and confusion seems
to be the only constant.

Every thought is an enigma,
burdening, swarming, pulling;
I don't know which way to turn.

Any attempt I make to
determine a direction
towards growth, towards life,
is thwarted; I'm on a leash
extending only as far as my
thoughts allow.

So, I fan to flame the flickering truth:
The dark will always try to choke out the light,
for it knows once light enters in,
everything transforms.

I lean into this direction—
taking a chance on the belief
that things will get better.

It will get better,
it will get better,
it will get better.

But immediately I'm met with:

Will it?
Will it?
Will it?

My path through starts to
become more tumultuous,
toxic thoughts cycle faster, quicker,
swelling and swarming
to a claustrophobic state.

I see the pattern—
when dark thoughts see a sliver of light,
it threatens their home, so they try
and fight back with more chaos.

But I take the weapon of intention,
and kill these thoughts that made
up my past self. I revolt against them,
telling them they have no home here.

The chaos starts to soften,
as the light begins to leak in,
and residual darkness dissipates.

a poem for when you need a fresh perspective

Standing in the rubble
of what once ruled my mind,
I'm met with a clean canvas,
and all that matters —
an overwhelming peace,
stillness, and power over my thoughts.

rezan noelle smith

it only takes one
—

One after another
rejection, rejection.

My shoulders—heavy
my breathing—shallow.
It only takes one, it only takes one,
I tell my tender heart.

And one finally came.
It was better than I thought
much better than I deserved.

In the end, it did only take one.
Patience unfolded into a deep
sigh of relief, and the heaviness left.

a poem for when you need a fresh perspective

present

The pain of the present is overwhelming,
paralyzing, but I'll usher in hope
by taking notice of the small:

fireworks embodied through blooming flowers,
the soft cotton knit sweater against my skin,
decaffeinated Earl Grey tea.

And though I don't see them, I hear them—
the birds, and I know hope is the same.

Here.

regan noelle smith

name day
—

My eyelids depart softly
from the base of my eye.
This next year of life
slips in lazily.

So goes the start—
a season of anonymity,
forgotten for a while, while I
prepare my heart
in the quietest of places.

I won't see a change today
but will reap in plenty,
for this tough season
could be avoided,
delayed by distraction,
self-ended.

But I choose to press into it,
to allow a cocoon to weave
around me tightly, careful
not to break the shell prematurely.

Reminding myself,
that though the cocoon is dark,
it is not dangerous,
it is not an entrapment—
rather a quiet preparation,
where my trust is tested,
and where time unfolds
a grand amelioration.

a poem for when you need a fresh perspective

fruition to come
—

At first glance,
the bare branches
seem locked in winter's spell—
a quiet shock of cold.

But look more closely:
tiny buds have begun,
foreshadowing the fruit
that summer will bring.

You bring blue jay lovers
into view, chasing one another
through budding branches.
The cardinal, brilliant and blazing red,
makes my heart leap.
The hawk glides down, wings wide,
and lands atop the Sugar Maple tree.

All of this reminds me—
You care, even for the sparrow.
And my fruition will come, too.

A poem for when you are feeling joy.

These words will celebrate with you.

a poem for when you are feeling joy

alacrity
—

Alacrity!
There it is!
A cocktail of energy
and joy within me!

Mental peace;
in June we bloom,
in July we burst
in the best way;
a bright outpouring of
sparks, energy,
alacrity.

There it is!
Alacrity!

regan noelle smith

sun shaped eyes
—

My soul cheers in
cartwheels and somersaults
on a bed of jubilee,
covered in gratitude,
a blanket of contentment,
now tucked beneath my toes.

I exchange air with a smile,
seeing magic in the mundane,
and even in the plain there is
beauty, sweet surprises that are
vast and varied.

I dance from treetop to treetop,
snatching a handful of buds.
My head is in the clouds,
thoughts are tangled in the
trees.

This scene isn't serendipitous,
it's been carefully considered,
thoughtfully constructed.

There's no wonder You
saw this and called it good.

a poem for when you are feeling joy

how dreams deepen
—

Pauses on the red rock trail to experience the evergreens—in both sight and scent. Morning tea and blanket writes when the early air bites. Late night talks with my mom. Solo traveling. Seeing someone's eyes light up when sharing their passion. Patiently waiting for tea to steep in a quiet home. Long walks to nowhere, with conversation about anything.

regan noelle smith

joy is here

Grief may be prevalent,
but joy is ever-present.

It may not take on the
expression of cartwheels or carousels,
but the warmth of an immovable and
internal joy remains.

a poem for when you are feeling joy

big joy in small things
—

I love it when:

squirrels run across along the
top of the wooden fence with
acorns in their mouth

a bird carries
long grass from her beak

my dog slowly paces away with an
empty peanut butter jar in his mouth

birds soar in airport interiors

I get to move and stretch my body in a barre class,
refuel with brownies and prosciutto sandwiches

I spend time with my love, the pure play of putt putt.

What small things fill your heart with big joy?

regan noelle smith

orcharding
—

Since the sun offered its summer
serenity, chrysanthemum fireworks
have been bursting within me —
butterflies of inspiration and creativity
have been tumbling together in the pure
blue sky, and my heart and my mind feel
whole for the first time.

I've stayed consistent as the moon's cycles,
within new routines and abandoned ones.

Provision abounds;
I pluck perfectly ripened peace and joy —
there's more fruit than my two arms can carry.

Long walks in lavender fields, pausing
during picnics to pray; I pen poetry often and
delight in this balance.

My obedience and Your goodness
has been building together, unfolding
into something even more vast
and otherworldly than these orcharding trees.

a poem for when you are feeling joy

alum creek forest
—

My head lays limp on a bag full of books,
with my mouse-brown hair webbed with the
surrounding switchgrass stems.

On a sheet sprawled out in the forest,
my eyes face the tree's canopy,
the sunlight freckles through.

Cotton-like tree seedlings mid-flight,
oh how they magnify this light,
gossamers gracefully gliding with gravity.

An ethereal experience,
a revelatory venture,
for all is soothing, settling, affirming.

Banal as it may seem to some,
it is true bliss to me.

joy
—

Tell me about your clementine joy.

Hold it close to your heart;
others may try to smolder it out—
saying it's too vast or too else minute,
but it's just their heart yearning to
feel the same.

You have chosen to see through
the lens of beauty and wonder and
awe, living life with vivid eyes.

So tell me about your clementine joy,
so I may share in it with you.

a poem for when you are feeling joy

the beat of jubilee
—

I place my hand over my heart. My palm feels my
pulse. I close my weary eyes, but my heart remains active.

beating beating beating

It's not slow like the drone of a lo-fi drum, nor does it
have ongoing echoes from a mallet to a gong; this beating
isn't like a hummingbird heart; rather, it's steady—

beating beating beating,

And with its rhythm, my mind's eye synchronizes with
the ripples of rain on water, and sunbeams spread like
liquid onto my arms; surging through my veins,
security is as sure as the sustained

beating beating beating.

A poem for when you need to grow.

A warm invitation, these poems will encourage and stretch you.

a poem for when you need to grow

i will be
—

May I be one,
who loves with action, grace, and truth,
who gives so generously,
that even when it's done in secret
it's still evident.

My I be one,
who is safe to process and share with,
even when a thought or idea is
partially formed, premature
or opposes my own.

May I be one,
who listens with great attentiveness,
whose company is like a warm embrace,
and who shares both laughter and hardships, alike.

regan noelle smith

metamorphosis
—

You don't need a sign
to awaken and self-reflect.
You don't need a cue
to start living more aligned
with who you are.

You don't need permission
to quietly refine your: character, heart, mind—
to build yourself a hidden chrysalis,
to give yourself to a cycle of metamorphosis,
to shed your past skin as you rebuild
yourself with truth.

Without all eyes watching your growth, the
world may see you as dormant,
but in due time, you will emerge with an
undeniable transformation.

And you don't need a sign to make this
metamorphosis cyclical within yourself,
or to encourage it in another—but if
you *want* permission, may this poem be
that invitation.

a poem for when you need to grow

cycles
—

I've lived in cycles before,
trapped—by my own resistance
to feelings and facets of life—
in a circle of circumstance, and
I've handled my current state
as though I was my past self.

I choose instead to sync with a new rhythm,
to rewrite the phases of a cycle I can sustain;
I notice every feeling and every
facet of my being, clearing out the clouds
in my blue-sky consciousness to make room for
this challenge I choose to see as an opportunity:

I allow feelings to flow through, and
whatever encounters of déjà vu,
I decide to either execute
false impressions to their death, or find
and honest feeling—and make room.

My trajectory may intersect with my past self,
but only for a second; for it's traveling further and
further towards the eastern sun.

regan noelle smith

a challenge to the self
—

When will you stop staring into space,
wondering when you will act, what you will
make of this life—the sacred gift of time.

Take this minute;
yes, this very moment to act;
ask for discernment,
but be filled with action,
rather than being stifled
by waiting for direction;
you were born to be empowered.

Your very soul was constructed
with divinity; you share the same spirit
with the God that watches you
through the clouds,
through even the thick of your head,
through your sticky mess of a mind,
through all you fear, your frozen steps—
step now, and act on your yes.

a poem for when you need to grow

heart's posture
—

You see me
here and now
my whole intention
through a lens of
eternal perspective, and though
my misconceptions may fall
like scales from my eyes
with time, you don't fault me
for that today.

Instead, you see me
with honest and loving eyes,
a love that wraps my whole heart,
and gently whisper the ways I can grow,
encouraging and with a strong voice,
rejoicing in who I am.

Here and now.

precious

—

A variation on The Summer Day by Mary Oliver

With my one wild
and precious life:

I will listen well,
walk slowly and live unhurried.
I will take time to greet and rub
the cat bearing its orange belly.

I will quiet the world in my mind
to meditate on scripture. I will boldly
build others up while not making myself small.

I will offer space to hold deep hurts,
and have a heart that surrenders them.

I will change,
I will grow,
I will always be learning.

I will seek out You, Lord—
consistently, daily, even when I
don't hear a word back—because
I will notice Your beauty when
I slow down
long enough
to rub the cat's orange belly.

a poem for when you need to grow

surrender
—

Search the corners of your
heart to find hope, and hold on.

Outpour in love, serving those who
least expect it.

Surrender all control—even what you
hold close—exchanging it for trust and freedom.

let us never give up

The One who is intimately familiar
with all our flaws never gives up on us—
so I will not give up on myself, or you, either.

When I glimpse your hurting heart,
folding like lemon-lime prayer plant leaves at dusk—
quiet, protective, retreating from the world—
aching, even if misdirected,
may I extend grace.

And while sometimes this grace looks like
quiet prayer, honest conversation, or distance
for a short time—may you receive from me
the same unconditional love I know—
one that restores and redeems.

a poem for when you need to grow

flawed heart
—

May I never follow
my own flawed, fickle heart—
an unknowable guide.

Though free to lead,
I choose discernment,
trusting not myself
but Your quiet voice.

In Your presence,
my heart renews,
finding strength
beyond my understanding.

shift
—

You are where you're meant to be;
and when you feel it in your bones
that you are not—shift.

a poem for when you need to grow

paradise
—

Paradise to me has become less
about sunsets and traveling and seas,
and more about mindfulness in the
sacred in-between—

in the very space I find myself today.

reminder

Give yourself permission to write—
especially if it's only for you.

a poem for when you need to grow

daytime dreams
—

Nighttime terrors of long-ago memories;
I wake up in a fog, hazy yet frozen,
but take a breath and realize
I determine the dreams of daytime.

So even if your night has been cloaked
with a starless sky, as an act of courage—
let us choose joy.

regan noelle smith

steady

Settling into the foreseeable future
feels unsettling. It's reminiscent of
a past season, when complacency
and laziness plagued. But in this
rhythmic familiar, it's a season
        of   steady.

Because I've lived days
when the next minute, day,
week was unpredictable—
a rollercoaster of adrenaline
in a survival mode state.

I remember craving steady then.

Shuffling between crisis and chaos,
whiplashed to routine and
recovery.

There's something simple
in the stillness, a sweet
contentment—but only if I
choose to be—
                            steady.

a poem for when you need to grow

i'm still called to steward
—

Rainwater, inspiration.

The creek is what I steward.
It all trickles together to
create a waterfall—impact I
may or may never witness.

May I keep my sights focused
on the greater purpose.

vapor
—

Life is hazy and brief;
more time is not a guarantee.
So we must stay focused,
live undistracted,
fill our time with
of purpose and passion:
increasing our impact,
decreasing ourselves,
resting in restorative waters,
drawing from a deep well.

a poem for when you need to grow

nostalgia
—

What my heart desires,
isn't always what's best—
I've seen it tumble back
into habits that make it sick.

Nostalgia
can be a disease,
starting small then taking over
everything; nothing will ever
be like it once was.

What once was,
was never perfect anyway,
though with distance its glow
is iridescent.

Today turns over
to create the past we'll soon
romanticize; let's not lose sight—
of the only time we can hold.

floating
—

I hold myself responsible
for the actions of others.
For things I cannot control.
Weight
         ed.
Tethered to unrealistic,
unattainable standards.

It's become too
         heavy.

Reluctantly
leaving my lips, I whisper
I am only responsible for my own conduct.

Slightly louder, I whisper a prayer and
surrender; my hands unclench.

I'm freed from this undue responsibility.

The contrast makes me feel like
I am floating, and I find the weight was never
truly mine to hold.

a poem for when you need to grow

good things
—

What if you lived
as though you truly believed
all the good things said about you?

regan noelle smith

questions for real answers
—

I ask the questions I wish
someone would have asked me:

Are you okay?
How are you feeling, really?
What are you excited about at this moment?
What are your passions and most daring dreams?

I get to ask, and I hear the pleasure
of vulnerability spilling; external processing
for the first time; and their passion unfolding,
giving a look into the life they wish to lead.
I see them come alive, either in raw human
brokenness or raw human joy.

It's an honor to share in their
authentic emotion.

I don't wait for others to ask,
so I'll ask myself:

Are you okay?
How are you feeling, really?
What are you excited about at this moment?
What are your passions and most daring dreams?

a poem for when you need to grow

trajectory
—

I try to choose the thoughts that take me
into an upward slope of living, something
so steep I think I'm bound to slip off.

Sometimes I do, too; I either stay in a
state of stagnation, or dip downwards
towards death—even if the drop spots
were once high points for me.

Because that's the thing about
trajectory—it has nothing to do
with where you've been and
everything to do with where you'll go.

open hands

My hands are tired.

Rug-burned and raw, I've been
playing a subconscious game of
tug-of-war with memories rooted
in the past, trying to pull them
back into the present's possession.

But I know I must let my
hands lay limp, allowing them
to be empty—empty and ready
to welcome change
with open arms.

a poem for when you need to grow

gratitude stream
—

Gratitude is the water I use to snuff negativity, for I've learned by now, even a small spark of negativity can grow ablaze like wildfire so hungry yet so all-consuming. I want to align my mind to come back here to this moment where my head is settled on this sole topic: nothing else matters except the flow of this stream of consciousness. It doesn't quite feel like it was self-derived, though it moves seamlessly through me, and maybe that's why You brought me here: to teach me what gratitude looks like.

expanding
—

Like any other muscle
that must tear to build strength and expand,
my heart must break.

Let it break for what breaks Yours.
I want it to tear and rip to
increase in its capacity.

I want to grow my empathy
and pump more of this lifeblood.
I want to comfort others, even if
it may eclipse my own comfort
in effort to hold another's heart
more gently.

I want to stay tender, soft.
overflowing, outpouring,
becoming a haven for others to
process their hurt; to heal.

a poem for when you need to grow

i'm here for you
—

Grow without me,
but know my door is always open.

I couldn't come up with the right words,
but maybe there weren't any words that
could have met you when your heart was
heavy and your voice weak.

I hope you step into your purpose,
even if I never have a hand in it;
I'll be thrilled to see it, even from afar.

I'm rooting for you.
I'm here for you,
in whatever capacity you'll let me.

A poem for when you need rest.

May these poems prompt you to pause.

a poem for when you need rest

take care
—

I wasn't taking care of myself.
I was neglecting my needs,
surrounding myself with people and
depleting what little left I had to offer.

My skin wore my inside's anguish,
I had trouble entering into a state of slumber,
though once I settled there, I struggled to leave.

I wrapped myself in work,
hoping it might keep me from drowning, but
instead, it slowly cut off my circulation.

Then in solitude, I decided
to mend myself, allowing the quiet to
clear room for my grieving,
letting go of the distractions and disappointment.
I let myself dance, sing; I let myself solely be.

This is what I needed to recharge:
an empty room—a cleansing sight for a messy mind,
slowly unwinding, peace prevailing, my thoughts,
finally, free to pass by.

empty
—

You can't pour from an empty cup, but I've been bone dry for a while with no well or reservoir for miles. I'm tired. So tired. So spent and sick but pressing through. Late nights and shallow sleep. God sees me here. I think He may have overestimated my strength, but I know He's always good. He hears me, for silent tears are prayers, too.

Silent tears are prayers, too.

a poem for when you need rest

take the time
—

I can take time today to rest.

Work will always be there.
Even what is urgent
can be made to wait.
Everything will be okay.

I can take time today to rest.

meditate
—

Constantly humming, now overheating
my mind struggles to settle
in the midst of this chaotic contemplation.

Though I feel far from peace,
I meditate on my thoughts, noticing
as they come and as they go; it's less
watching them whirl and more
watching them pass. I try not to
unravel them or determine their root.

I simply notice, and become
a witness to my breathing.

a poem for when you need rest

morning's mourning
—

Nudged awake,
the sun and moon both sat in
the celestial dome they call home;
the moon had not yet
slipped away, the sun just started
to progress above the horizon.

In my morning's mourning, You
met me. You whispered powerful truths
gently, always in my most
fragile moments.

regan noelle smith

simple acts of rest
—

My spirit has been gently
pulling me to rest; it knows
that when I'm fatigued, I'll
start to pick at my emotional scabs.

I lean into my spirit's prompting and

go on a walk,

look out at nature,

call my siblings,

meditate,

read a book,

or simply slow myself long enough
to watch the water boil and amber
plume from the tea bag as it steeps.

a poem for when you need rest

cafe st. jorge
—

A blue coffee shop
littered with little ships and white borders,
postcards free to ship and share.

I've been learning to still myself,
an act I continuously am refreshing,
reworking,
rebuilding.

My natural state leans towards
racing a thousand miles an hour
with a million thoughts flying,
raging—
a spaghetti mess of a mind.

I watch a woman edit photos,
another quantify metrics,
my eyes meet a man
rubbing his knuckles together,
I notice how my finger lingers off the pen.

I sit within this space.
I am.
I know.
I trust.

The front door is swung wide open and propped
but despite the bustling city,
it only allows one entry at a time.

regan noelle smith

I want to be the wide opened door—
open to all but able to funnel a
s i n g l e
awakening consciousness at a time.

a poem for when you need rest

let us be lilies
—

We are meant to live
like the lilies which lay
together in the valley;
they are bold, unabashed,
and do not compare nor
compromise their beauty.

Field grass reaches perfect
peace in fully being itself and
evening air can hold so many hues—
each one a marvel.

How much more beautiful are you,
even as you're simply existing,
breathing, loving.

regan noelle smith

butterfly box
—

I have had my metamorphosis,
but there will still be seasons,
I'll retreat to my butterfly box —
a home to hibernate, to rest, a space
of safety to simply be.

a poem for when you need rest

A poem for when you crave awe.

Because life is a great gift.

a poem for when you crave awe

i don't have the words
—

I feel myself missing
the elegance my words once held,
now a mess of experiences,
raw and unpolished;
some things can never
fully be captured by any
arrangement of letters, things like:

>the sheer excitement
>and nervousness held in the eyes
>of an incarcerated woman who
>received her date of release
>after years of not seeing
>her family in the outside world

>>the sweet sound of waves folding
>>atop themselves during rush hour
>>when rubber tires tread against
>>the rough highway road

>>>the independence of walking
>>>Spanish streets alone at night

>>>the realization I'm struggling
>>>with veiled pride and the
>>>simultaneous gratitude and
>>>disappointment that emerge

>>the fragile heart fighting
>>through tears to say that
>>my words helped them feel
>>less alone

regan noelle smith

      the generous gift, absolute
      joy, and shifting challenges
      of marriage

There's a special sentiment
in some things never having
quite the right words
to describe them.

a poem for when you crave awe

the beach
—

My eyes drift along the coast
with the pull of the tide,
constant and constantly moving;
I see beings along the beach—
scattered like sand.

Each comprised of their own
reflections, deductions, and musings.
Accompanied by their family
and other sunseekers.

They are you and they are me,
splashing upon the shores—
I think about how, in a way, we are
alternate variations of each other—
all a different lens made in the image
of our Maker, influenced, shifted, eroded
and built by our past, perspectives, and
environments.

Basking within the sunlight,
bathing in the ocean.

I wonder while I walk the waterfront,
seeing them smile and splash upon the shoreline,
if they catch that this current moment is as brief as
the ocean foam curling along the waves—
and if they hold it close.

rezan noelle smith

commonalities
—

The sun that shines through my
window's wooden slats and onto this page
is the same sun that brought light to your
morning, and tucked itself beneath the horizon,
as you began to settle into your night.

When you feel
isolation slip into your scene,
set your sights
on all we already share:
soak in the stretches of sunlight
savor the sliver of our same moon,
delight in the same Big and Little Dipper, too.

Even the water we drink or dive into
flows from me to you and back again,
repurified since it was first separated
from the sky.

I may not know what your
heart carries today,
but leaning on the beams
of these commonalities,
I know our loads are lighter.
We have more in common
than we'll ever come to know.

And in a way, we have each other.

a poem for when you crave awe

this hour, heaviness lifted
—

The air feels lighter in this afternoon hour, and living,
loosely entering my lungs and graciously descending.

The sycamores have burst into bloom,
morphing into leaves now swaying—
where green meets blue,
gentle, simple hues.

Oh the grandiose of green,
layered through all foliage and trees, and how the birds sing;
their tender temperament rings out in me, too.

The leaves sing and sway, active—
with the warm wind carried from the west,
their soft underbellies glisten—
golden, golden.

Aglow with a light that is alive.

regan noelle smith

love story
—

The sun slowly sinks
down into the horizon,
as if she's about to drown herself
into the ocean; a sea breeze blows,
and pages slap my hand, a reprimand
for writing such a morbid phrase.

I can't help myself,
for this very scene —
the interaction between the wind, the waves,
and beaming light — has been my muse since
I was young and painting watercolor sunsets.

The gale and sun are close lovers.
I see him weeping from her grand,
golden goodbye; she'll soon be
gone for the night.

I see the stars congregate, holding hands,
strung along above the ocean waves,
and as the sun departs, they hurry
to take their place in the indigo sky.

It's sweet how the lovers embrace together,
the wind and the sun; she's nearing the end
of her sweet, deep red song,
just as she arose this morning;
and now with notes of heavy lavender,
almost fuchsia, turning grey, then blue,
she completely slips away,
praising her Creator in some distant place.

a poem for when you crave awe

The only sound left
is the whisper of the waves—
I've always marveled at how they
harmonize with this scene, a repeated
rhythm reflecting the sun's parting song.

The deep blue has fully encompassed,
the clouds have changed their tune,
the wind has even stopped for a moment,
then proceeds to take a deep breath—
restless for the rest of the night,
until the sun returns again in the morning.

And while I no longer paint this
scene with paper and brushstrokes,
I sing its song as I fall asleep,
when my breath becomes too short,
winded in my own way,
or when I simply want to remember:

the light always returns.

the day bids adieu
—

My anxiety quiets,
humbled by the grace of this view.

A myriad of colors gaze
into my eyes—teal trickling
into peach, slipping softly
into blood orange,
embracing like long-lost lovers.

Whitecaps sway onto the shore—
a beauty language can't quite hold,
though man will endlessly try.

a poem for when you crave awe

sandstone shadows
—

The bones of this mountain
reach up to the heavens, pine trees
laid throughout the land.

The birds have white breasts
and black beaks, they leave
their nests in the red rock's
pockets to meet me.

Gliding against the jagged
edges and the pure blue,
they find me in the cavity
carved from the wind and
rain's gentle erosion, as if
they've made this space
especially for me.

We sit together and sing
our songs—sound waves
echo off the rock, crystal clear.

And once we've finished,
I stumble out and watch
them soar—drifting from
boulder tip to tip, their
spotty shadow spills over
the juniper and white fir trees
until the shadow steadies,
for it has met the smooth
sandstone surface below.

regan noelle smith

water droplet
—

Have you had the honor
of reaching every landscape on the earth,
penetrating through the limestone hearts
filtering through even the deepest parts of the earth?

Have you had the pleasure of
congregating, creating a cloud
community in the sky, holding
the reverence of the sunset, caressing color,
or reflecting it as a part of an ocean wave?

Have you known the touch of the ocean floor,
flowed between species unknown,
been a safe space to let them live, to let them be, to let them
simply float, swim, scurry.

Have you ever rolled down a rushing river,
tumbled into the air then dove onto stones
to create a soft soundscape —
or been given the opportunity to be hidden,
frozen within the arctic, or the last drop of ice
that needed to morph and melt, freeing
a glacier to glide slowly down
a mountainside.

a poem for when you crave awe

multi-dimensional
—

Your love is not a circle, but a sphere:
the first, the last, and multi-dimensional.

regan noelle smith

california sand dunes
—

A silent shore.

Sand swept into human-sized ant hills,
and as for us —
we look like ants, too.

Small little specs within this space
our problems,
how they slip through our fingers.

Blessings roar,
in sequence with the
depth of the ocean.

Shuffled speckles of
sugar, salt, turmeric, black pepper
grains slip down
the curve of the dune's spine,
settling below,
always making space,
windswept together,
hills and valleys.

And the sky,
oh the sky —
it's covered by a cloud
who boldly interjects,
stretching from horizon to horizon,
a translucent and gentle gray,
as if to say:
Look how big your world could be.

a poem for when you crave awe

safe house
—

Humans,
each with their own thoughts
and hurts and homes; I wonder
where they take shelter.

I wonder if they retreat to
their own head and heart and
skin and bones, if they look to
others, look to the heavens, or
if they look to the mountains,
asking for meaning time can't erode.

generous promise keeper

Generous promise keeper—
even the ones whispered
are fulfilled with lavish wonder.

a poem for when you crave awe

picasso museum
—

Cockatoos setting the scene,
my feet walk the Spanish streets
and linger in the Picasso Museum.

Human expression; family and home
recurring themes.

Picasso and I both
make art like our fathers—
infused with perspective,
layered with psychological insight.
Again and again, his drawings—
and my writing—bring us
back to our father.

Roses painted on wood; inspired
by Van Gogh. My eyes decipher
the marine blue monochromatic
display as it's met with a deep
red hue. I don't need an x-ray
to know that there's more to this
piece; the depth has already
pulled me in by both my shoulders.

wonder
—

What else do I think I understand, but
        instead, I'm completely mistaken?
Oh, how I've most often mis-sized the
        magnitude of my Maker. So vast
        and absolute; gentle and steady.
Now, I humble myself;
        I'm simply a speck floating through
        time and space. Yet Your
Distance is not distant despite my depravity
        in disposition to Your divinity.
Even in my conscious disobedience and my
        deep valley lows; You're here with me.
        You always have been.
Readily, You entered our world—wholly God,
        dwelling in humble human frame,
        enduring this duality until death to deliver me,
        and in a radiant resurrection you rose again.

        I'm overwhelmed with awe; all that's left is
        to respond with gratitude, worship, and great

Wonder.

a poem for when you crave awe

alley cat books
—

Among my ventures
of self-driven stature,
my feet fumble upon a bookstore
and in the back
I hear a reading.

A beautiful array of individuals together,
I sit discreetly in the corner
to listen in on the blend of generations.
Middle-aged men, young women, teachers,
and those still with curfews.

One woman with charcoal hair,
red-lips and large golden earrings
motions to me, and points
to the seat beside her, like she's
been awaiting my arrival.

These souls have all gathered,
to bare, collectively, each other in the form
of in-progress poetry, memoir manuscripts,
short fictions, pure prose.

Eagerly they listen to viewpoints and
opinions from vast perspectives.
They humbly collect the slips of paper with
pencil-written words, like treasure.

A blank slip of paper is passed
to me bidding for my opinion—
to write my personal words of
encouragement and critique.

A British man with thick-framed glasses
and messy grey hair speaks to the group,
a professor and moonlight panel moderator.

A girl with chocolate curls shares her story,
of cosmic space romance, black holes and
time space continuum. She must
have shared this chapter before,
for she received such praise
for the revisions she's made.

Another author shares of autonomous-vehicle
kidnappings, a future scene laid atop the
San Francisco setting we sit in now; he
seemed to want the practice of reading aloud,
over feedback from strangers.

An old woman reads of air-trains
travelling back into the past
in efforts to offer the possibility of
a conversation with a cancer-killed sister;
the room was mostly quiet at the
end of her reading, soaking in
the words, holding back tears.

On occasions when I lay
in a sunny patch of grass,
and the light blinds me,
even with my eyelids shut,
I think back to that old woman
and wonder if she ever got her
draft just right.

a poem for when you crave awe

in my neighborhood
—

Everywhere I look I see You:
we've made a museum of memories
together in this temperate weather, sharing
slices of watermelon, spitting seeds down
by our feet.

We hear laughter of the suburban children—
a collage of color and abundance of joy.
You delight in their joy, too.

You've been helping me learn my capacity
and how it increases whenever I lay my burdens down
and carry Your empowerment. I hold tightly to nothing
aside from the promise You've generously given.

deep well

A love like water,
morphing and changing,
taking different forms,
evaporating, circulating,
pooling together,
reflecting, saturating—
but never absent,
never dry.

a poem for when you crave awe

seattle
—

Forget by Shallou plays in the foreground
as seagulls scream in the distance; we whisper
sweet nothings from our seats
in a bougie BMW SUV.
I scratch his hair
in tempo with the tune.
We watch the clouds dance
through the sunroof, and talk
about how tall these trees must be.

I tame my hair in a top knot to stop it from
the whipping wind and admire
yellow blossoms lining the road shoulder.
Lethologica is an unknown or forgotten word,
not unlike its meaning and purpose,
but I refuse to forget this.

I consciously un-wrinkle my brow in rebellion
to the bright sun. Riding downhill,
a freeing feeling with a bit of reckless joy.
Momentum pushes us forward.

We find the beach is unfit for camping
and haul our belongings back, but before we do,
we sit in the sand, watch the frothed milk waves
erode the black rocks.

gift

Some gifts
prove so honoring
and honest
and selfless,
you can only receive them
with little expression
and a tear
that quietly falls.

I've felt this way many times:
Receiving a sunset painted across the sky,
a framed drawing of a favorite art installation,
forgiveness that holds the weight of the earth.

Some gifts
leave us wonderstruck.

a poem for when you crave awe

A poem for when you are feeling (or seeking) gratitude.

We'll share in this, together.

a poem for when you are feeling
(or seeking) gratitude

that consistent question
—

I pose the question
I've asked my mirror reflection
for the past decade:
Are you happy with who you have become?

When I was sixteen, I whispered in the night
that I wouldn't see my twenty-first birthday
due to a death of my own cause,
whether that was
an overdose of substance or
the absence of food or
dark thoughts causing my own undoing.

But I am standing here, still.
Strong and tall, learning each day to love the
bones and body I was born into,
knowing I was created for a purpose.
This moment held sacred,
when I can say with confidence:

I'm happy with who I have become.
My life alive with breathing lungs
that lose their breath from laughter,
with arms that hold those I love
and a voice that declares freedom
and breakthrough.

This story, these words, I now share
with another sixteen-year-old girl who
whispers to herself in the night
of the surprise, gratitude, and joy —
when you wait and work for that worthy *yes*.

vessel
—

I am thankful for this body—
a vessel in which I'm able
to see the world, feel the
world, walk the world.

I'm sorry for ever hating it—
the temporary carrier of my spirit.

For this is where life quite
literally manifests—
where my thoughts take shape
and turn to actions; it's where
I feel, breathe, dream, connect, create.

And it allows me to experience
this life where amidst and despite
struggle—beauty abounds.

a poem for when you are feeling
(or seeking) gratitude

even every crumb
—

We were fed full on
favorable conditions;
continually repeated, they
now seem tasteless, stale.

As we progress through the
day-to-day, fragility sets in to
our emotions, and we're shattered
by the smallest imperfections or
alterations of our expectations,
all consuming and bitter to our tongue.

But then tragedy awakens.

Stunned and taken completely off guard,
the soggy ground grips at our ankles.
Nearly paralyzed but still absolutely
free, our previous problems seem trivial.

At our most vulnerable state,
the self uncovers all.

I've despised my former self,
wishing I had noticed how the sun shined
upon my face—regretting that I'd find shade
instead of basking in the rays.

Even still, our current tragedy is another's
dream; their world falling (or already fallen)
apart.

While not discounting the challenge
we may face, we start to admire anything,

well, admirable. Appreciation
overtakes us with every bit of air
inhaled, every flavor savored.

We live in the present. Expecting little
yet outrageously grateful for any and all
provision. Our eyes uncovering more and
more the more we look around. And now,
regardless of our current standing, we value
everything.

Every provision becomes a
monument of gratitude.

a poem for when you are feeling
(or seeking) gratitude

peonies, again
—

My dad sent me photos of my mother's peonies today,
their buds beginning to bloom in her backyard
botanical garden.

That car conversation with my dad reminded me how
grateful I am I exist;
and I'm grateful that I feel grateful to exist.

Last year's peonies and I were left a mangled chaparral—
between the deer picking off our blooms of joy, and the
deep snow of cold circumstance crushing.

But in this year's growth the goodness is full, and our
flowers are so significant, we kiss the earth. The rich aroma
of our resilience is worship.

And so, alike this year's peonies, my joy,
my gratitude, and I join in bowing to our Creator.

gratitude

I extend my arms out,
parallel to the soft soil,
and with my eyes that
help me see more than
what's in the scenic scope
now trace these long limbs
down to my fingertips —
these are the hands which
cradle my head, interlock
with others', and dance
when I speak.

My arms and mind
wrap love around this
home, for I could have
been made to be a
wandering spirit, or
simply the air, existing
between the branches of an oak.

a poem for when you are feeling
(or seeking) gratitude

may 25
—

I hear the red cardinal call,
singing the song of today,
alongside the occasional hum
of a modern-day machine.

I'm practicing open awareness,
the simplest form of gratitude.

To acknowledge
everything in existence,
and to soak in all surroundings.

I look at what's ahead,
along with each fuzzy-faint fragment
happening within my peripheral.

I'm amidst a stagnant scene—
neighbor boy, not even four years of age,
playing with airplanes while a maintenance
man fixes another's air conditioning.

Recognizing it all,
without label or thought.
Solely existing,
gratitude inevitably following.

Little pieces of tree pollen fall
on my head and tangle in my hair.
Alternating bees linger around my yellow mug,
filled to the brim with hot turmeric ginger tea.
The breeze picks up and releases more pollen,
gravity pulling it to ground.

Grounded. This is where serenity dwells,
within the stillness. My tired mind
has finally been emptied of its clutter and clamor,
and now is solely taking up space.

I get lost in this space,
buried in gratitude.

Amidst this blank scene,
anxiety isn't able to erupt
in any form nor capacity.
Standing still with a wide-lens view,
encompassed by my surroundings.

I'm allowing myself to hear, feel, breathe.

*a poem for when you are feeling
(or seeking) gratitude*

prolonged solitude
—

Prolonged Solitude is the only one
who has created such a space to where
my claustrophobic subconscious can
finally take a deep breath, reach out and
pen itself to paper.

Prolonged Solitude has given me
revelations and understandings of myself
in ways I've never known before;
she's been honest and kind and has
kept me accountable.

Her silent words have shown me
myself in raw and uncomfortable ways,
where I realize I've been storing
shattered glass in my side—only
now my eyes aren't too busy to
see it, my hands aren't too busy to help,
and my schedule isn't too full to alleviate and heal.

I've mistaken her for danger before,
long ago, when we weren't well acquainted.
I mistook her as an enemy—
and thought I responded with
purposeful neglect, but when I numbed
her out, it was because I was screaming—
trying to fill the void which would
only leave me with a sore throat and
a messy mind. I inaccurately
attributed that character to her.

For while she's a quiet friend—
one who says few words—

those few words are pure wisdom,
always bringing me back to myself,
to still myself, to slow my thoughts,
to remember who I am when I am
not busy, and for that. I am thankful
for her—Prolonged Solitude.

*a poem for when you are feeling
(or seeking) gratitude*

stillness
—

In the stillness, I see many birds
scampering about, making homes in
the shrubbery, singing harmonies together—
the lavender leaves cast shadows on stone,
a doe and her fawn,
look at me with wide eyes.
I meet them with wide eyes, too.

Their white speckled bodies,
taking it all in,
for it's the first time they've seen me—
and it feels like the first time, I'm
truly seeing, too—
I take a sage bush and break a sprig
beneath my fingers and massage it
into my palms.

In the last bit of daylight, I shed
a tear for this scene, with a heart
full of gratitude.

regan noelle smith

interconnected
―

I've always said that
poetry is a divine art—
a mirror, a lantern, a bridge—
it's why I think so much
of scripture is written in verse,
not just simple script.

It's an unobstructed lens
straight into the heart,
that can be received
just as soberly in reading.

Interconnected,
you to me.

So thank you for sharing
your sacred moments
of vulnerability.

May these small, written
words echo something already in you—
true each time you return.

about the author

Regan Noelle Smith is a writer, speaker, and poet based in Columbus, Ohio. Her work explores grief, healing, and emotional honesty, guiding readers toward transformation through truth and spiritual insight.

Having faced mental illness and past drug abuse, Regan has found poetry and vulnerability central to her own healing. She inspires women to grow through poetry and leads workshops in halfway houses, using writing to process trauma, reclaim stories, and build community.

Rooted in lived experience, her writing resonates deeply with women navigating emotional complexity and personal growth.

Other books: *Morning Air, Morning Light / Cloudland*
Website: *regannoellesmith.com*
Instagram: *@regannoellesmith*

www.ingramcontent.com/pod-product-compliance
Lightning Source LLC
Chambersburg PA
CBHW020932090426
42736CB00010B/1118